AIR POWER

Antony Loveless

Tick Tock

An Hachette UK Company
www.hachette.co.uk

First published in Great Britain in 2008 by TickTock, a division of Octopus Publishing Group Ltd,
Endeavour House, 189 Shaftesbury Avenue, London, WC2H 8JY.

www.octopusbooks.co.uk
Copyright © Octopus Publishing Group Ltd 2008

All rights reserved. No part of this work may be reproduced or utilized in any form or by any means, electronic or mechanical, including photocopying, recording or by any information storage and retrieval system, without the prior written permission of the publisher.

ISBN 978 1 84696 718 4

A CIP catalogue record for this book is available from the British Library

With thanks to series editors Honor Head and Jean Coppendale
Thank you to Lorraine Petersen and the members of nasen

Printed and bound in China
10 9 8 7 6 5 4 3 2 1

Picture credits (t=top; b=bottom; c=centre; l=left; r=right):
Aaron Allmon II/ U.S. Air Force/ Reuters/ Corbis: 4-5. Richard Cooke/Alamy: OFC (plane). AFP/ Getty Images: 5b, 11t, 29b. Getty Images: 11b. Antony Loveless/Crown Copyright: 1, 2, 6, 7, 8-9, 9t, 12-13b, 14, 15, 16-17, 18, 19, 20-21, 22, 23t, 23b, 26-27, 27t, 28, 29t, 31. Kyle Niemi/ U.S. Coast Guard/ ZUMA/ Corbis: 10. Shutterstock: OFC (background), 24, 25t, 25b. Katrina V. Walter/ U.S. Navy/ Reuters/ Corbis: 13t.

Every effort has been made to trace the copyright holders, and we apologize in advance for any unintentional omissions. We would be pleased to insert the appropriate acknowledgments in any subsequent edition of this publication.

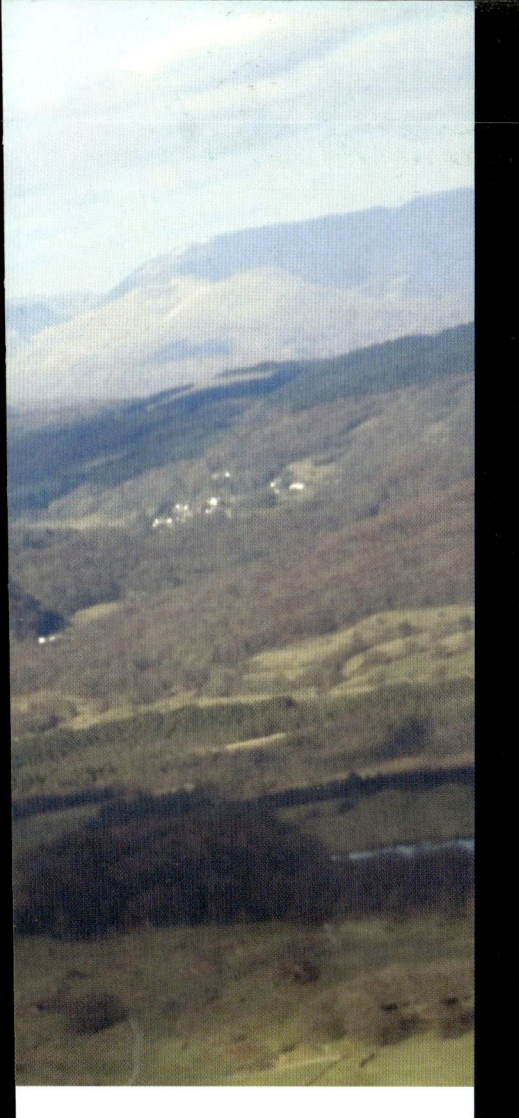

Contents

Chapter 1
Air forces at work.............4

Chapter 2
Quick Reaction Alert.........6

Chapter 3
Emergency help..............10

Chapter 4
The pilots......................14

Chapter 5
The aircraft 22

Need to know words 30

Pilot training/
Air forces online 31

Index 32

CHAPTER 1
AIR FORCES AT WORK

In a war, soldiers on the ground need protection. They need protection from enemy planes. This is the job of the air force.

The air force shoots down enemy planes. Sometimes it bombs enemy planes on the ground before they can take off.

F15E Strike Eagle

Air-to-air missile

The Royal Air Force (RAF) has 1,000 aircraft. The United States Air Force (USAF) has over 6,000 aircraft.

When not at war, the air force's job is to stop air attacks on civilians.

An attack could come from enemy aircraft, or from terrorists.

Air forces also help people affected by natural disasters such as floods and earthquakes.

May 2008 – Supplies are loaded on a USAF plane for cyclone victims in Myanmar.

CHAPTER 2
QUICK REACTION ALERT

One important area of work for the RAF is "Quick Reaction Alert" or QRA. If a plane is hijacked, or something unusual happens, fighter plane crews are ready to react.

Controller

Every minute of every day there are thousands of aircraft flying in UK airspace.

At an RAF base, controllers watch the signals sent from aircraft. The controllers also watch for enemy planes flying into UK airspace. If the controllers see something unusual, the fighter plane crews are told to "stand by". This is QRA.

6

As the pilots run to their planes, ground crews prepare the planes for a quick take-off.

Pilot

Every second counts!

"Our day lasts for 24 hours. We do one day on, one day off. We live in our flying gear. We sleep fully kitted up. It saves time if we have to scramble."

QRA pilot

Within minutes of the QRA, the jets are flying. The fighter planes can accelerate at up to 2,470 km/h – this is twice the speed of sound.

The pilots fly close to the enemy aircraft to see how dangerous the threat is. Then they report back to the people in charge on the ground.

Typhoon F2s

If terrorists took control of an airliner, they could fly it into a city. Many people might be killed. The air force would have to shoot down the airliner.

Tornado F3s

"We're trained to kill fellow pilots in the air. There's huge respect amongst pilots, even on opposing sides. But at the end of the day, we have a job to do. It's us or them."

QRA pilot

CHAPTER 3
EMERGENCY HELP

The USAF and RAF don't just fight wars and terrorists. They also help around the world when there is a major emergency.

In 2005, the city of New Orleans was flooded when Hurricane Katrina hit the USA.

Here, a CH-47 Chinook helicopter drops giant bags of sand. Water is flooding streets and houses. The bags will hold back the water like a barrier.

The USAF rescued people who were trapped in the flooded city.

12

Air force men and women also helped on the ground. They looked after people who were hurt. They cleared blocked roads and helped to rebuild homes.

A C17 transport plane loaded with supplies to help the tsunami victims.

CHAPTER 4
THE PILOTS

When not at war, fighter pilots perform QRA duty. They also fly training missions called "sorties".

Sorties include low-level flying and pretend air-to-air battles. A training flight will be two to four hours long.

A normal day will also include intelligence, weather and weapons briefings.

Making pre-flight checks before a sortie.

"Every time we get airborne, we do something to make us better pilots. There is always a point to the sortie."
Fighter Pilot Sam Cowan

Flying gear

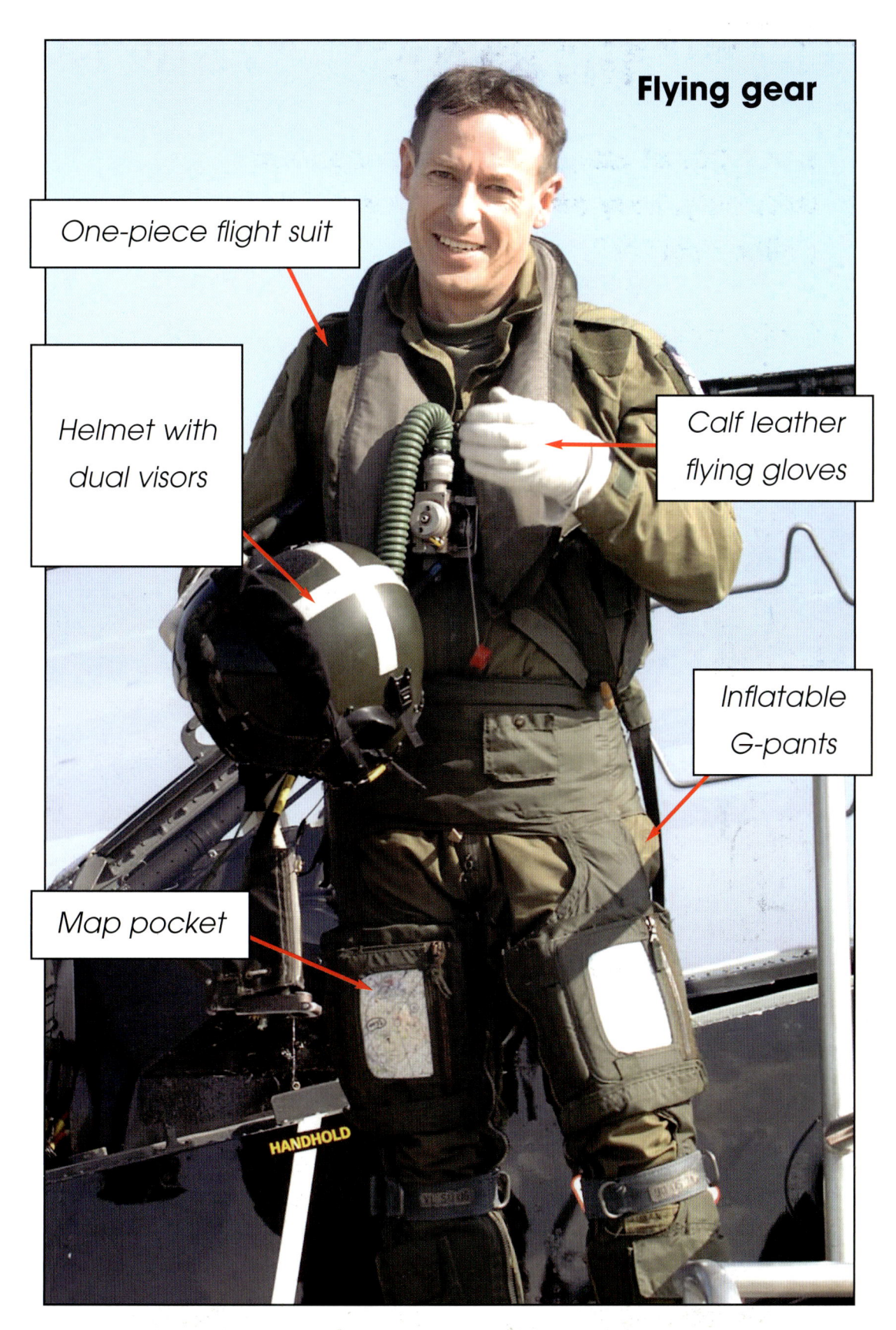

- One-piece flight suit
- Helmet with dual visors
- Map pocket
- Calf leather flying gloves
- Inflatable G-pants

" Everyone who flies fighter jets feels lucky. When you walk to your aircraft, it's awesome. You might think I haven't been supersonic for a while, so you will do that. Having that power at your fingertips is just amazing."

Fighter Pilot Sam Cowan

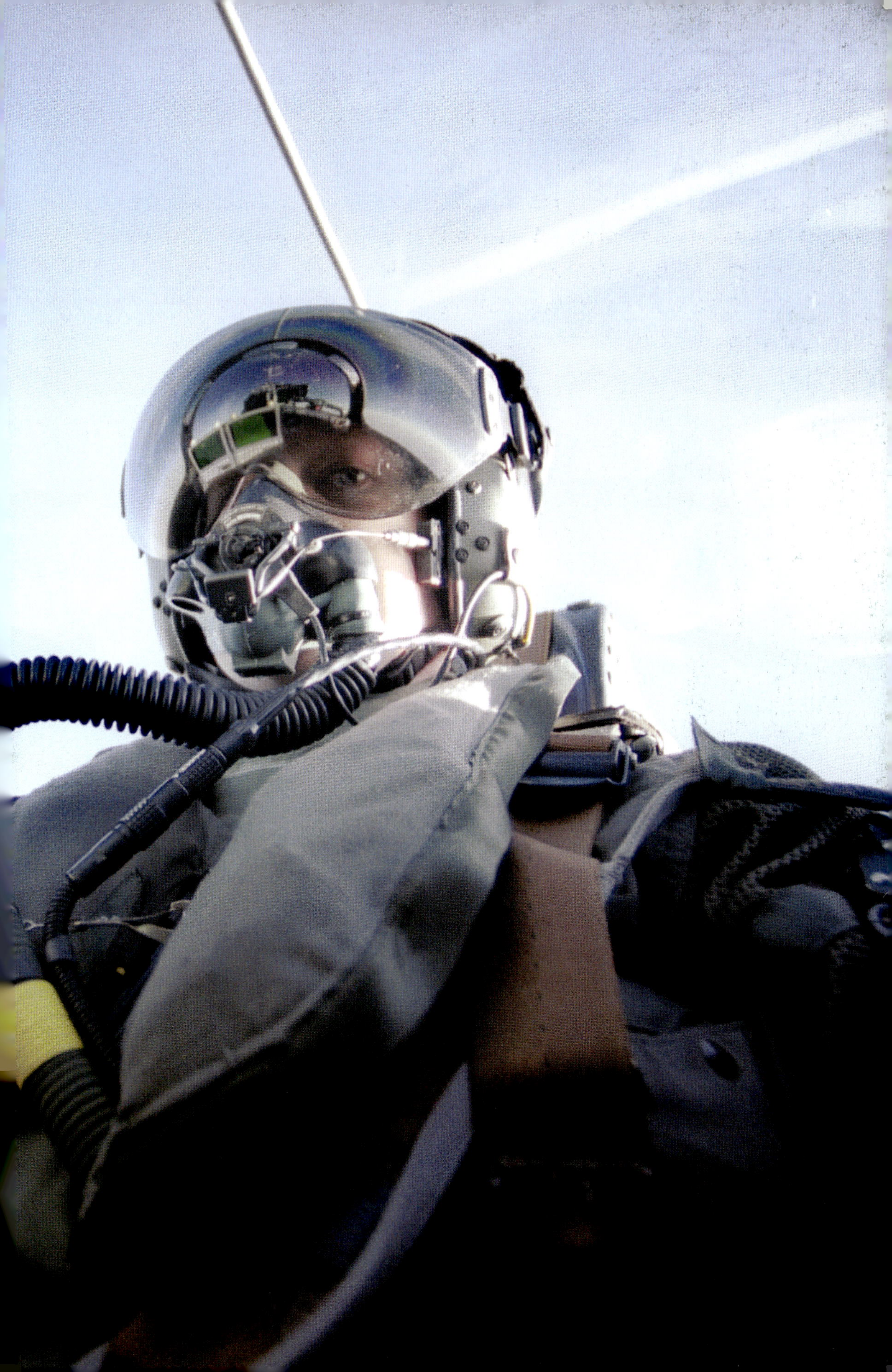

Pulling a tight turn at low-level.

Unlike airline pilots, air force pilots are trained to fly at low levels.

This is so they can fly planes under enemy radar. Low-level flying is fast and very dangerous.
It needs to be practised regularly.

All the flying is done by the pilot. There is no help from computers.

The pilot is flying at 11 kilometres per minute. The plane is just 46 metres off the ground.

The smallest mistake could mean certain death for the pilot!

Low-level Tornado F3s

Pilots must learn to cope with g-force.

G-force is what you feel when you hurtle down a rollercoaster. The g-force on a rollercoaster is about 3g. For a fighter pilot it can reach up to 9g.

As g-force gets higher, it affects the pilot's body. Blood is dragged to the pilot's legs and feet. This could kill the pilot. Special trousers called g-pants help to stop this.

Next to go is peripheral vision. This means the pilot can't see out of the corners of his or her eyes. It's like looking down two toilet roll tubes.

Finally, everything turns black and white. The pilot may pass out.

As g-force gets lower, the pilot's senses return to normal.

Dual tinted and clear visors protect the pilot's eyes

Microphone on/off switch

The breathing regulator supplies oxygen. High up, the air is too thin to breathe.

Oxygen hose

CHAPTER 5

THE AIRCRAFT
Typhoon F2

The RAF's newest aircraft is the Typhoon F2. It is the most advanced fighter jet in the world.

Each plane costs about 60 million pounds!

The F2 can climb 1.2 kilometres into the sky within 30 seconds of take-off.

It can cruise at supersonic speeds and travel at 9g during supersonic moves.

In air-to-air combat, a fighter pilot must keep his or her eyes on the fight at all times.

Visor

The F2 has a sight-activated missile-firing system. This means the pilot can fire missiles at a target just by looking at it!

Typhoon F2 cockpit

The F2 computer sends information about fuel and altitude onto the pilot's visor. This means the pilot doesn't have to look down to check the cockpit instruments.

Instruments

23

F-22 RAPTOR

The F-22 Raptor is an American fighter jet. It is used to attack and bomb enemy targets on the ground and in the air.

The F-22 is armed with six air-to-air missiles.

F-22s cost almost two hundred million pounds each!

The F-22's top speed is over 2,500 km/h.

25

Fighter jets need to be light and fast. This means they can only carry enough fuel for 60 to 90 minutes of flying. Most sorties last longer than this.

A Combat Air Patrol (CAP) can last for hours. This is when fighter jets patrol an area looking for enemy aircraft. They must destroy the enemy planes before they reach their target. Air-to-air refuelling allows the fighter jets to stay in the air.

Large planes act as airborne fuel tankers.

Fighter jets waiting for fuel and those that have been refuelled, protect the tanker plane.

Tanker plane

Basket

Hose

Fuel is delivered using a basket-like piece of equipment on the end of a long hose.

Jet taking on fuel

27

The USAF and RAF use lots of different support aircraft during wars and rescue missions.

CH-47 Chinook helicopter

The CH-47 Chinook is a twin-engine, heavy-lift helicopter. Its main job is moving troops and supplies to battlefields.

The Chinook has a wide loading ramp at the back. Supplies can be dropped from the ramp.

Ramp

The Hercules C-130 is used to transport troops and equipment. It is also used to rescue people from dangerous areas.

Hercules C-130

The Hercules can do short take-offs and landings using very rough runways.

NEED TO KNOW WORDS

accelerate The rate at which a plane increases its speed.

airspace The air (sky) above a country in which aircraft can fly. Each country controls its airspace and says which aircraft can fly there.

altitude The height of an aircraft above the ground.

briefing Giving accurate information to the pilots about a situation.

civilian A person who is not in the air force, army or navy.

co-ordination Being able to make your body and senses work well together. For example, when a pilot's eyes see danger, the pilot's hands must react fast on the aircraft's controls.

cruise To fly for a length of time at one speed.

ground crew The non-flying members of an air force. They take care of the aircraft.

hijack To take over and control an aircraft by force.

intelligence Information about the enemy or enemy activities. It is usually secret.

radar A way to detect distant objects. Radar can work out an object's position and speed by sending radio waves that reflect off the object's surfaces.

scramble Quickly enter an aircraft and fly somewhere in response to an alert.

stealth technology Technology that makes an aircraft almost invisible to radar. A stealth plane has special panels which absorb radar waves instead of reflecting them.

supersonic A speed that is greater than Mach 1 (the speed of sound). Mach 1 is about 1,238 km/h.

victim A person who is hurt, killed or affected badly by an event.

PILOT TRAINING

Becoming a trainee
- To be given a place as a trainee pilot, you must have excellent exam results. You must also be fit with good eyesight. Pilots also need above average co-ordination skills.

This is the pilot's view in a Hawk aircraft simulator.

Training
- Pilots train on full-motion flight simulators. The simulators handle andrespond exactly the same as real aircraft. However, the trainee pilots don't have to leave the ground.

Non-flying jobs
- Most air force jobs are on the ground. There are hundreds of non-flying jobs that keep each pilot and aircraft in the air. These jobs include air traffic controllers, mechanics, cooks, medics and drivers.

AIR FORCES ONLINE

Websites

http://www.raf.mod.uk/
The RAF's website

http://www.raf.mod.uk/careers/jobs
Find out about careers in the RAF

http://www.eurofighter.com/
All about the Eurofighter Typhoon

INDEX

A
air-to-air missiles 4, 24
air forces 4-5,
aircraft 22-23, 24-25, 26-27, 28-29

C
C17 transport plane 12-13
CH-47 Chinook 11, 28-29
Combat Air Patrol (CAP) 26

E
emergency help 5, 10-11, 12-13

F
F15E Strike Eagle 4
F-22 Raptor 24-25
fighter planes 8-9, 22-23, 24-25, 26-27
flying gear 7, 15
fuel 26-27

G
g-force 20
g-pants 15, 20
ground crews 7, 30, 31

H
Hercules C-130 29
hijacking of planes 6, 30
Hurricane Katrina 10-11

L
low-level flying 14, 18-19

N
natural disasters 5, 10-11, 12-13

P
pilots 6-7, 8-9, 14-15, 16-17, 19, 20-21, 31

Q
Quick Reaction Alert (QRA) 6-7, 8-9, 14,

R
radars 19, 24, 30
Royal Air Force (RAF) 4, 6-7, 8-9, 10, 12-13, 14, 22, 28

S
scrambling 7, 30
sight-activated missile-firing system 23
sorties 14
speed (of planes) 8, 22, 25
stealth technology 24, 30
supersonic speeds 16, 22, 30

T
terrorists 5, 9
Tornado F3s 9, 19
training 14, 19, 31
tsunami (south-east Asia) 12-13
Typhoon F2s 8-9, 22-23

U
United States Air Force (USAF) 4-5, 10-11, 12-13, 14, 28

V
visors (helmets) 15, 23